1

Fumita
Yanagida
Presents

TOMO-CHAN IS A GIRL!

CONTENTS

A Once-in-a-Lifetime Misfire

I WASN'T EXACTLY SUBTLE.

JUN!

I LOVE YOU...

AS SOON AS I GOT INTO HIGH SCHOOL I, AIZAWA TOMO, CONFESSED TO THE GUY I LIKE.

BUT I'M CLEARLY A GIRL!

SO, UH... HOW ABOUT IT, HUH?

PEOPLE SAY I'M "LIKE ONE OF THE GUYS"...

THIS IDIOT...

TOMO!

WHAT ARE YOU SAYING?

BUT THIS GUY...MY CHILDHOOD FRIEND, KUBOTA JUNICHIRO...

NEVER TREATS ME LIKE ONE!!

Y-YAY... HA HA...

FIST BUMP

BRO!!

Yeah~!

I LOVE YOU, TOO...

3

Skirt Shock

SO WE'VE PLAYED TOGETHER SINCE WE WERE KIDS.

ME AND JUN ARE NEIGHBORS...

WE WENT TO SEPARATE SCHOOLS ALL THROUGH ELEMENTARY.

KUBOTA HOUSEHOLD

AIZAWA HOUSEHOLD

BUT EVEN THOUGH OUR HOUSES ARE RIGHT NEXT TO EACH OTHER, WE WERE IN DIFFERENT SCHOOL DISTRICTS.

JUN LOOKED AT ME IN MY UNIFORM AND THE FIRST THING HE SAID WAS...

WE'RE FINALLY IN THE SAME SCHOOL!

Mornin', Jun!!

......

WE WERE FINALLY TOGETHER WHEN WE REACHED JUNIOR HIGH.

THAT WAS WHEN I FIRST REALIZED JUN THOUGHT I WAS A BOY.

Wha?!

DON'T YOU THINK THE SKIRT'S A LITTLE MUCH?

What a way to come out.

HEY...

4

A Natural Touch

MORNIN', TOMO~!

Eek?!

BAP

FLINCH

HE DOESN'T MEAN ANYTHING BY IT, BUT...

DID YOU SEE THE SOCCER MATCH LAST NIGHT? It was amazing~!

JUN PULLS THIS CRAP ALL THE TIME.

WHAT'S WRONG? Your face is red.

HUH?

shake shake

THIS JERK...

OH, BY THE WAY, I DO KARATE.

THE HELL?!

OOF!!

MOR... NIN'!!!

THUD

5

Too Close for Comfort

WHAT'S UP, JUN?

HUH?

CLOP

CLOP

HEY! HEY, TOMO! LOOK AT THIS!

JUN NEVER THINKS ABOUT PERSONAL SPACE...

HEY...

SQUEEZE

LOOK AT HOW HIGH HE JUMPS FOR THIS DUNK!

I FOUND THIS AWESOME VIDEO.

NOT MINE, ANYWAY.

WH-WHOA.

BA-THUMP

BA-THUMP

HERE IT COMES! RIGHT HERE!

HE GETS THE PASS AND...

NEVER EVER!!

SQUISH

BEE BEE BEEE~!!

BOOM! SEE?! AWESOME, RIGHT?!

Is he for real?!

6

Ignoring the Headlights

WH-WHAT?! B-B-BRA?!

JOLT

I WONDER IF IT'S TRUE.

I HEARD FROM THIS GUY WITH A GIRLFRIEND THAT BRAS ARE HARD TO TAKE OFF.

BUT I'M PRETTY SURE HE KNOWS I'M A GIRL.

I ALWAYS WEAR A SPORTS BRA, SO...

I-I DUNNO...

JUN TREATS ME LIKE ONE OF HIS MALE FRIENDS...

BA-THUMP

BA-THUMP

WELL, I'M SEVENTY PERCENT SURE...

HUH?

WHAT?

HE JUST FORGETS, NOW AND THEN... I THINK.

......

YOU WEAR ONE?

OH... OHH, RIGHT!

7

Misuzu-chan, An Honest Friend

YOU KNOW, TOMO...

SAY SOMETHING, MISUZU!

To him, I mean!

JUN'S SUCH AN IDIOT! HE'S ALWAYS TREATING ME LIKE A GUY!

SO I'LL GIVE IT TO YOU STRAIGHT: YOU EARNED THIS.

I'VE KNOWN YOU BOTH FOR YEARS...

BUT YOU NEVER PLAYED HOUSE OR DOLLS WITH ME IN KINDERGARTEN, NOT ONCE.

AND I ASKED YOU A MILLION TIMES...

YEAH, FOR PAY-BACK...

YOU FOUGHT A LOT WITH OTHER KIDS IN JUNIOR HIGH, RIGHT?

B-BUT JUN ALWAYS ASKED ME TO PLAY...

HOW MANY TIMES DID I SAY, "PLAY WITH BOYS ONLY IN MODERA-TION"?

S-SOR-RY.

RANT

RANT

GET WHAT?!

GET IT?

THIS IS WHY EVERYONE TREATS YOU LIKE A GUY NOW...

SOME- TIMES I WANT TO, BUT...

WELL...

DO YOU THINK OF ME AS A GUY TOO, MISUZU?!

THE HELL ?!

HUH? WHAT DO YOU MEAN?

UNLIKE JUNICHIRO, I HAVE A YOUNG WOMAN'S PERSPEC- TIVE...

NOT REALLY, NO. I'M AROUND YOU TOO MUCH FOR THAT.

High School Changing Rooms

Junior High Field Trip

OH, JUST I'VE SEEN THINGS...

WHAT PARTS OF ME DO YOU THINK ARE WOMANLY?

PLE- ASE SHUT UP.

WHAT? REALLY?! YOU THINK THEY WILL?

I don't really get it, but...

SOON ENOUGH, OTHERS WILL SEE YOU AS A WOMAN... AS I DO.

Changing Your Tune

YOU'RE LOUD.

LOUD...?

I CAN'T JUST START SPEAKING ALL GIRLY...

Y-YEAH, BUT...

FIRST OF ALL, THE WAY YOU TALK IS NO GOOD.

OH, RIGHT! I MEAN... VERY WELL?!

LIKE THAT.

HELL YEAH!

TRY BEING A LITTLE LESS BLUNT, OKAY?

HOW ABOUT WE START BY SPEAKING A LITTLE SOFTER?

HUH? SOMETHING FEELS OFF...

OH, GOSH, UH...

Let me think...

Ha ha...

FOR LUNCH?

I got a yakisoba roll.

DID YA BUY LUNCH, TOMO? WHAT DID YOU GET?

Prac-tice.

A-AN OLD...

MAN?!

YOU SOUND LIKE AN OLD MAN!

WHAT'S WITH YOU?

AH HA HA HA!

Same Fight, Different Motives

JUN COMES AT ME LIKE I'M JUST ANOTHER GUY.

I COULD SAY THE SAME TO YOU!!

HUH?!

HUH?!

WHAT'D YOU SAY, JERK-FACE?!

ME AND JUN FIGHT SOME-TIMES.

LET'S GO, PUNK!!

FLINCH

GRAB

COME AT ME...

EEK ?!

SO LET'S GO!!

C'mon!

YOU TOLD ME TO COME AT YOU!!

Hey!!

YANK

STOP ...

HUH ?!

WH-WHOA... TIME OUT...!

THE FIST-FIGHT GOT WORSE FROM THERE.

GWAM

I SAID STOP IT!!

Root of All Evil

I GOT MY LICKS IN, BUT THAT RIGHT HOOK OF HIS...

I'M HOME...

THAT FRICKIN' JUN... HE HIT ME HARD.

JUN-BOU?! YOU DIDN'T LOSE TO HIM, DID YOU?!

I COULDN'T POSSIBLY WIN!!

I-IT WAS JUN...

AH!

Ack. Dad...

HEY, TOMO!! WHAT HAPPENED TO YOUR FACE?! WHO HIT YOU?!

YOU TAUGHT HIM KARATE, TOO!! AND I'M A GIRL!!

WHAT'D YOU SAY?!

Huh?!

DON'T BE STUPID!

DON'T TALK LIKE THAT!! YOU'RE THE NEXT LEADER OF THE AIZAWA DOJO!!

YOU'RE THE ONE WHO BROUGHT ME UP LIKE THIS!!

SHUT IT, OLD MAN!!

WHAT?!

This is all your fault!!

RRRAK!

GET CHANGED THIS INSTANT AND MEET ME IN THE DOJO!! I'LL BEAT THAT ATTITUDE OUT OF YOU!!

Peace Talks

AND BESIDES, I GOT HIT MORE THAN YOU.

Look at my face.

Hmph!

SHLRP

COME ON, TOMO. YOU STILL MAD ABOUT YESTERDAY? I SAID SORRY...

WHAT'S GOING ON WITH YOU?

· · · · ·

What's up?

SLIDE

SHLRP...

YOU'VE BEEN PUNCHING ME A LOT LATELY.

SPEAKING OF...

I KNOW YOUR WEAK SPOTS!

FLINCH

TICKLE TICKLE

I'LL GET YOU TO TALK!

Talk to me! ♪

COME ON, TOMO!

IT'S BECAUSE OF THIS CRAP!!!

BAM

Deep Bromance

Bounce, Bounce

LOOKS LIKE TOMO PUNCHED HIM.

THEY HAD A FIGHT...

GROOAAN...

TRUDGE TRUDGE TRUDGE

HE'S BACK.

YEAH!

The Next Day.

SHE GOT HIM GOOD AGAIN.

GROOAAN...

TRUDGE TRUDGE TRUDGE

WHAT IS HE MADE OF? RUBBER...?

YEAH!

The Next Day.

TOMO-CHAN
IS A GIRL!

Door Number Two

ME TOO.

OH...

I GOTTA HIT THE BATH- ROOM.

You go on.

CREAK...

I DIDN'T REALIZE YOU WERE GOING TO THE GIRLS'.

WELL, I WAS JUST FOLLOWING YOU...

WHY THE HELL WOULDN'T I?!

WHAT ARE YOU DOING IN HERE?!

Tomo-chan's Routine

YOU AND JUNICHIRO ALWAYS COME TO SCHOOL TOGETHER.

YEAH.

HE PICKS ME UP EVERY MORNING.

YOU'RE ALWAYS TOGETHER AT SCHOOL, TOO.

I GUESS.

SO WHY DO YOU ONLY HAVE LUNCH WITH ME?

WELL...

I KNOW JUN **WANTS** TO EAT WITH ME BUT...

A GUY AND A GIRL HAVING LUNCH TOGETHER IS...

KIN-DA...

IT'D LOOK LIKE WE WERE DATING?

IT'S A LITTLE LATE FOR THAT!

Sticking in My Craw

Tomo-chan's Growing Up

ARE YOU KIDDIN' ME?

WHAT?!

THE TWO OF YOU ALREADY LOOK LIKE A COUPLE.

JUST TELL HIM.

D-DO MORE...?

BUT DON'T YOU WANT TO DO MORE?

YOU'RE ALWAYS TOGETHER...

SO I DUNNO...

BLUSH...

A LOT W-WOULD CHANGE IF WE WERE LOVERS, RIGHT...?

WELL, YOU KNOW...

YOU'RE THE PERV!!

I-I'M NOT!!

PERV.

Daydreams

AND THE WEATHER'S SO GOOD TODAY.

SO MATH IS NEXT? Boring!

I NEVER REALLY THOUGHT ABOUT IT BUT, IF WE WERE TO START DATING, OUR CURRENT RELATIONSHIP WOULD CHANGE...

I CAN'T IMAGINE IT AT ALL...

I WANNA RUN AROUND OUTSIDE~!

WOULD JUN AND I *KISS*?

YOU'RE SPACING OUT.

FLINCH

Eek?!

HEY, 'SUP?

THE HELL?!

GUU┼!

GON

22

Swing and a Miss

FINE, JUST CALM DOWN.

JUST TELL ME!!

OW...

WHAT'S IT TO YOU?

HUH? MY TYPE OF GIRL?

SHARE MY INTERESTS, TOO.

I DO!

SHE'D HAVE TO BE ATHLETIC.

THAT'S ME!

I GUESS... I LIKE TALL GIRLS MORE'N SHORTIES.

I'M TALL!

I'LL JUST GROW IT OUT!

NO PROB!

AND I LIKE GIRLS WITH LONG HAIR.

CLENCH

I DON'T.

HOW 'BOUT YOU? WHAT KIND OF GIRLS DO YOU LIKE?

Shoulder-Length Tomo-chan

I LOOK PRETTY GIRLY, RIGHT?!

Heh heh!

I GREW MY HAIR OUT.

HE CAN'T CALL ME A GUY ANYMORE!

GLANCE

JUN SHOULD HAVE NOTICED BY NOW...

BA-THUMP

NO WAY!! REALLY?!

WHA...

YOU'RE LOOKING GOOD LATELY.

A SURF... DUDE?

SO COOL!!

LIKE A SURFER DUDE!

WHAP

24

Cleaning Up

WELL, HE *IS* AN IDIOT.

MY HAIR FINALLY GREW OUT!!

DAMN IT!

THAT MOUTH-BREATHER JUN SAID I LOOKED LIKE A SURFER DUDE!!

A-A MESS?!

ACK!

YOU LOOK LIKE A MESS.

YOU CAN'T JUST GROW YOUR HAIR WILLY-NILLY.

YOU NEED TO PICK A STYLE.

I DON'T KNOW WOMEN'S HAIR-STYLES...

WHY WOULD I...?

DO YOU HAVE A HAIRSTYLE YOU WANT TO TRY OUT?

I ENDED UP CUTTING MY HAIR.

THAT WOULD RUIN OUR FRIEND-SHIP.

TRA~LA~LA~

I GUESS I'LL TRY THE SAME AS YOURS...?

Boxed In Together

HUH?

OH, THIS?

HEY, TOMO, WHAT'S THAT?

?!

BUT STARTING HIGH SCHOOL'S A BIG DEAL!

I DON'T DO IT THAT OFTEN...

OHH...

IT'S A PHOTO-BOOTH THING I DID WITH MISUZU.

NO... NO WAY...!

WHAT?!

WHY NOT? WE'VE NEVER DONE IT BEFORE.

RIGHT?!

WE SHOULD DO THAT!

"I KNOW" WHAT?! WHAT IS IT?!

WHY ARE YOU ANGRY?!

HUH?!

B-BUT A GUY AND A GIRL DOING THAT TOGETHER IS...

You know...

BFFs

YOU'RE ACTING LIKE A KID...

I SAID WE ARE, SO YES!! It's photobooth time!!

ARE WE REALLY DOING THIS?

HEY...

Say cheese!

FLASH

THAT'S BECAUSE YOU WERE ALL OVER ME, DOOFUS!!

Huff... Huff...!!

YOU LOOK WEIRD IN EACH ONE!

HA HA HA!

DON'T YOU DARE!!!

Wha—?!

LET'S USE IT!

THEY'VE GOT A STAMP THAT SAYS, "BEST FRIENDS FOREVER!"

WHAT'S THE PLAN?

YOU LOOK SERI-OUS.

HE NEEDS TO REALIZE THAT I'M A GIRL.

I NEED TO STEP UP MY GAME WITH JUN.

HUH?

CLENCH

I'LL LET MY FISTS DO THE TALKING.

I'LL BEAT IT INTO HIM!

OH, SO *THAT'S* THE PLAN.

I SAID...

WHAT?

I'M SORRY ...

DOING THAT WILL JUST MAKE HIM TREAT YOU *MORE* LIKE A GUY.

SLOW DOWN.

ALL I KNOW.

JUN IS STRONG! BUT THIS IS...

OMAKE

A Natural Reaction

WHY'D SHE SUGGEST SOMETHING SO WEIRD?

DAMN MISUZU...

What I mean is...

COULDN'T POSSIBLY...

JUN AND I...

OH!

MUTTER MUTTER

?!

MORNIN', TOMO! WHAT COULDN'T WE POSSIBLY DO?

UWAA-AH!!!

WHY ?!

GUU!!!

THWK

Sports Reporting

WHAT DO YOU MEAN, "HOW FAR"?

HEY, TANABE.

HOW FAR HAVE YOU GOT WITH AIZAWA?

HEY, HEY, KUBO JUN!

MAN-AND-WOMAN ACTION...

HMM...

YOU KNOW... ROUGH, SWEATY, HOT MAN-ON-WOMAN ACTION! You can tell me! ♪

DON'T PLAY DUMB!

Soccer

Karate

SWEATY...

・・・・・・

WHAT?! SERIOUSLY?! No way!!

I GUESS WE'VE BEEN DOING THAT SINCE WE WERE KIDS.

Body Specs

YOU'RE REALLY INTENSE ABOUT THIS... What's your deal?

WHAT'S IT LIKE?!

HER BODY'S SO SLIM!!

IS SHE GOOD?!

Haah...

Haah...

WHAT DO I LIKE ABOUT HER BODY...?

THAT'S PRETTY HARD-CORE!!

LEG PLAY?!

HER LEGS! SHE'S REALLY GOOD AT USING THEM.

· · · · · · · · ·

I KNOW I ASKED, BUT SHOULD YOU REALLY BE TELLING ME THIS?!

WHY NOT?

AND HER HIPS! THEY'RE VERY STABLE.

YEAH, WE PLAY ROUGH.

NOT YOU, TOO!

OH... ROUGH PLAY?

JUNICHIRO WAS TELLING ANOTHER BOY ABOUT THE "ROUGH PLAY" YOU AND HE GET UP TO.

I'd say, "Boasting."

WHAT'S UP?

COME HERE.

WHAT'S GOT YOU WORKED UP?

HEY, TOMO.

WHAM

JUN! YOU JERK!!!

NOW I NEED TO EXPLAIN TO TANABE WHAT JUN REALLY MEANT BEFORE RUMORS START SPREADING.

WHAT A PAIN...

THWAK

Agggh!!!

YOU FRICKIN' MORON!!!

HUH? WHAT'D I DO?

YEAH! I'M FREE!

What's up?

HUH?! G-GUN-DOU-SAN?!

DO YOU HAVE A MOMENT?

TA-NABE-KUN.

I WASN'T PLAN-NING ON IT...

THAT'S WHY I DON'T WANT YOU SPREAD-ING ANY RUMORS.

NO.

SO, THEY'RE NOT GOING OUT?!

One short talk later.

WHAT, REALLY?!

JUNICHIRO DOESN'T THINK OF TOMO AS A WOMAN.

BUT THEY STILL SEEM LIKE MORE THAN FRIENDS.

Hmm...

THAT EXPLAINS WHY HE WAS SO WEIRDLY DISINTER-ESTED IN THE CONVER-SATION...

BUT YOU'RE STILL AN ASS.

STRICTLY SPEAK-ING, I AGREE...

GIFTED!

I don't get it!

BUT AIZAWA-SAN IS SO...

HINT HINT HINT HINT

Special Privileges

STRANGE...?

TWITCH

I DIDN'T REALIZE THEY HAD SUCH A STRANGE RELATIONSHIP.

OKAY, I KIND OF GET IT NOW...

DON'T YOU DARE.

I COULD GIVE THEM A PUSH... SOMEHOW... MAYBE...

SURELY AT LEAST ONE OF THEM HAS THOUGHT ABOUT IT!

HEH HEH HEH!

THEN LISTEN UP.

HUH? YEAH...

YOU JUST BECAME FRIENDS WITH JUNICHIRO RECENTLY, CORRECT?

AH!

OF COURSE! YOU DON'T WANT ANYONE MEDDLING IN YOUR FRIEND'S LOVE LIFE.

OH... S-SORRY!

O-OKAY?!

THE ONLY ONE WHO GETS TO MEDDLE WITH THOSE TWO IS ME.

Flew Too Close to the Sun

THAT WAY, I WON'T DO ANYTHING STUPID! AND YOU'LL HAVE A GUY'S PERSPECTIVE.

TWITCH

MI-SUZU... CHAN?

HEY, I KNOW! WHY DON'T WE WATCH OVER THEM, MISUZU-CHAN?

IT'D GIVE YOU MORE AUTHORITY... GREAT IDEA, RIGHT?

I'm here to help...

FIDGET

AND IT MIGHT BE EVEN BETTER FOR AIZAWA-SAN TO GET ADVICE FROM YOU IF YOU HAD A BOYFRIEND.

IT SUITS YOU!

OH! YOUR EXPRES-SION CHANGED!

WHAT ARE YOU TRYING TO SAY?

AH! S-SORRY. I'M GOING TO GO NOW...

NOT ANOTHER WORD.

STOP.

BUT IT'S NOT... AS GIRLY AS...

Levels of Devil

WHAT'S SO AMAZING ABOUT HER?

GUN-DOU?

SIGH~! MISUZU-CHAN'S AMAZING~! ♥

BUT SHE'S SO COLD AND HARDLY EVER SMILES.

BUT THAT'S PART OF HER APPEAL!

YEAH, I GUESS I CAN SEE THAT...

ARE YOU BLIND, MAN? SHE'S CUTE!

SHE'S LIKE A LITTLE DEVIL WHO JUST CAST A SPELL ON ME!

SHIVER ♥

THAT SHIVER SHE SENDS DOWN MY SPINE...

OH MAN... EVEN BETTER...

SHE'S MORE LIKE A GODDESS OF DEATH AND DESTRUCTION.

I WOULDN'T CALL HER A LITTLE DEVIL...

High Five!

THEN I COULD AT LEAST PUT MY ARM AROUND HER!

IF I CAN BE A GUY FRIEND TO AIZAWA-SAN LIKE KUBO JUN IS...

Heh...

MISUZU-CHAN SAID NOT TO MESS WITH THOSE TWO, BUT...

WAVE WAVE

AIZAWA-SAN!

WHAP

?!

?

WHAT'S UP?

NO-THING...

Ha ha ha!

TREMBLE

TREMBLE

YO, TA-NA-BE!

H-HEY...

38

Resource Scarcity

OH, JUN-ICHIRO.

WHAT SHOULD I...

TCH...

IT'S REALLY COMING DOWN.

SHAAA...

OH DEAR.

LOOKS LIKE THE WEATHER-MAN WAS WRONG TODAY.

HEY, GUNDOU. YEAH, I DID.

DID YOU FORGET YOUR UMBRELLA, TOO?

ME TOO.

I KNOW SOMEONE WHO CAN HELP.

SERVES YOU RIGHT.

YOU TOO.

APPAR-ENTLY SO.

WE'RE GONNA HAVE TO FIGHT OVER HER, AREN'T WE?

Childhood Memories

RUDE!

GO AWAY.

WHY ARE YOU EVEN *HERE*?

HOW DID IT END UP LIKE THIS?

IT'S FUNNY... ALL THREE OF US USED TO GET ALONG SO WELL...

YOUR IDEAS WERE ALWAYS THE BEST.

YEAH... WE USED TO PULL A TON OF PRANKS WHEN WE WERE KIDS.

IS THAT RIGHT?

THAT SOMEHOW ONLY TOMO AND I EVER GOT IN TROUBLE!

BUT I ALSO REMEM- BER...

It's Not Clear

I THINK SHE SAID KARATE CLUB.

YEAH...

SHAAA...

DOES TOMO HAVE CLUB AGAIN TODAY?

BESIDES, I'M DOING KARATE AT TOMO'S FAMILY DOJO.

I guess Tomo does too...

IT'S NOT FOR ME.

WHY DON'T YOU JOIN ANY CLUBS, JUNICHIRO? DON'T YOU LIKE EXERCISING?

KARATE'S BORING WHEN I CAN'T DO IT WITH TOMO.

HIGH SCHOOL KARATE IS SPLIT INTO A MEN'S AND WOMEN'S CLUB.

ABOUT WHAT?

ARE YOU SERIOUS?

SHAAA...

YOU...

41

Shut Up

IF TOMO GETS A BOY-FRIEND?

WHAT?

WHAT WILL YOU DO?

"YOU'RE MY WHOLE WORLD..."

HER FACE IS BRIGHT RED AS SHE SAYS...

TOMO SNUGGLING WITH AN-OTHER GUY, SOMEWHERE WITHOUT YOU...

YOU MUST HAVE THOUGHT ABOUT IT...

"I LO--"

SHO

VE

SHAAA...

She Really Is a Wingman

WHAT ARE YOU DOING HERE?

HUH?

DIDN'T YOU TWO GO HOME ALREADY?

FORGET HER, LET'S GO HOME TOGETHER.

HUH?

HUH?

SHAA...

WE BOTH FORGOT OUR UMBRELLAS.

A C K.

LET'S GO HOME!

M-MISUZU!

THAT'S WHY I'M TELLING YOU TO DO IT!

BEING UNDER AN UMBRELLA WITH HIM, THAT'D BE TOO INTENSE!

WHY'D YOU PICK ME?

Tanabe-kun's So Happy

A Girl's Smell

NO, YOU'RE NOT, YOU'RE GETTING SOAKED.

I-I'M FINE HERE.

HEY, COME CLOSER.

SHAAA...

HUH?

I DIDN'T NOTICE.

I WORKED UP A SWEAT AT KARATE CLUB, SO I STINK...

YOU ACTUALLY... SMELL REALLY GOOD...

ACK ?!

SNIFF

SNIFF

HEY! MORON!! DON'T SNIFF ME!!

YOU DON'T SMELL AT ALL.

TOMO ?!

H-HEY!

AHHH!!!

TMP TMP TMP TMP

45

He Went Home Like That

OMAKE

THE RAIN...

IS MY ELEMENT.

Slight Fever

HEY! Morn- ing...

GET A MOVE ON, TOMO!

HUH ?

You scared me!

WHY'D YOU TAKE OFF LIKE THAT YESTER- DAY?

· · · · ·

WELL...

UH, SURE.

DID YOU CATCH A COLD?

WHAT'S WRONG? HEAD- ACHE?

TOMO-CHAN
IS A GIRL!

The Person I Look Up To

SHE'S SUCH A WONDERFUL PERSON.

AIZAWA-SAN...

MY GODDESS...

SHE SWOOPED INTO THE KARATE CLUB THIS SPRING.

AND STRONGER THAN ANYONE!

SHE'S NIMBLER THAN ANYONE, SHARPER THAN ANYONE...

I GOT A LITTLE CARRIED AWAY...

I-I'M SORRY, MISAKI-SENPAI!

You all right?!

STRONGER THAN EVEN ME, THE KARATE CLUB PRESIDENT!

And By "A Little" She Means "Completely"

I'M SORRY ABOUT JUST NOW...

DON'T WORRY ABOUT IT!

THANKS, SENPAI.

Nice work out there.

WOW! YOU'RE STRONG AS EVER, AIZAWA-SAN.

I'M THE ONLY GIRL IN MY DOJO, TOO.

I'm used to it.

I'M FINE!

IT MUST BE HARD BEING THE ONLY GIRL...

ARE YOU USED TO THE MEN'S CLUB?

WHY DON'T I HAVE A WORD WITH THEM AND TELL THEM YOU WANT TO GO BACK?

I... I DON'T THINK SO.

WELL THEN...

TO BE HONEST, I LIKED THE WOMEN'S CLUB AND KIND OF REGRET LEAVING...

AIZAWA-SAN...IS UNBEATABLE EVEN IN THE MEN'S CLUB.

NO ONE WANTED TO TRAIN WITH ME AFTER THAT...

Ha ha ha...

IN THE MATCH TO CHECK THE SKILL OF NEW CLUB MEMBERS... I WENT A LITTLE... OVERBOARD...

Fear of Keeping Up

HOW DO I PUT IT...?

NOT EXACT-LY...

IS IT BECAUSE YOU WANT TO BECOME STRON-GER?

I HAVE TO SAY, IT'S KIND OF AMAZING THAT YOUR FAMILY RUNS A DOJO AND YOU'RE DOING KARATE AT SCHOOL!

THEY MOSTLY PLAY AROUND. IT'S REALLY LAID-BACK.

WHAT?!

STRETCH

WHAT'S THE KARATE CLUB AT SCHOOL LIKE?

TOMO'S GOT CLUB AGAIN TODAY.

Mean-while at the Aizawa Dojo...

YES, SIR!!

YEAH!!

YOU MUST HELP ME, JUN-BOU!!

RAAAHH!!

THEN SHE'LL NEED TO BE PROPERLY RE-TRAINED WHEN SHE GETS BACK!!

COMMON SENSE IS IMPOR-TANT...I GUESS?

ERM... WELL...

I FIGURED HERE I COULD LEARN COMMON SENSE.

I'M SCARED OF TURNING INTO A MONSTER IF I TRY AND KEEP UP WITH THEM ALL THE TIME...

A Difference in Values

I-I THINK YOU ARE!

STRETCH

I GUESS I'M JUST NOT VERY GIRLY, YOU KNOW?

I JOINED FOR A CHANGE OF PACE, BUT I WAS IN THE MEN'S CLUB BEFORE I KNEW IT...

Sigh...

BLUSH

AT LEAST, THAT'S HOW YOU APPEAR TO ME...

UUU BLUSH

YOU'RE AN AMAZING YOUNG WOMAN, AIZAWA-SAN...

HUH?!

Y-YEAH...

YAY!

AAHH

REALLY ?!

WHAT ?!

THAT'S THE FIRST TIME A GUY SAID THAT TO ME~!!

HEE HEE!

HEE HEE!

COULD AIZAWA-SAN LIKE ME...?

BA-THUMP

BA-THUMP

WOW, I DIDN'T GIVE HER THAT BIG A COMPLIMENT.

52

Words Cannot Describe It

53

Pep Talk

? SNIFF

YOU'VE GOT A LOT GOING FOR YOU, AIZAWA-SAN!

Lots and lots!

OH, THAT'S NOT WHAT I MEANT!

IT'S MORE LIKE... THERE'S NOTHING ABOUT YOU I WOULD CHANGE.

IT'S JUST, I DON'T THINK I COULD PICK JUST ONE THING.

YOU NEED TO HAVE MORE CONFIDENCE IN YOURSELF.

I THINK YOU'RE ALREADY AN INCREDIBLY CHARMING PERSON.

HE SOUNDS LIKE AN INTERESTING GUY.

RE-ALLY...

SO NOW I KNOW I'M AWESOME!

Ha ha ha

THAT'S WHAT HE SAID!

Hmm...

Go Away

Jun Really Can't Tell

I HEARD YOU MADE A NEW FRIEND AT KARATE.

YOU MEAN MISAKI-SENPAI?

I GUESS SENPAI'S THE ONE I TALK TO THE MOST.

MI-SAKI...? SOUNDS LIKE A GIRL'S NAME...

WHAT'RE THEY LIKE?

LET'S SEE...

I'M SURE I HAVE A PIC OF US ALL FROM OUR LAST PRACTICE MATCH...

AH, HERE.

THAT'S MISAKI-SENPAI.

ISN'T THAT A GIRL?

MISAKI-SENPAI'S GREAT! REALLY KIND AND SUPER NICE!

Well, That's All Settled Then

IS THERE A GIRL YOU'RE CLOSER WITH THAN GUNDOU?

HMM...

NO. WHY?

THOUGHT SO... I HATE TO ASK THIS, BUT...

WHAT WOULD YOU DO IF SHE FOUND A GUY?

SOMEONE SHE WAS HEAD-OVER-HEELS FOR, AND SHE STOPPED TALKING TO YOU?

I CAN'T IMAGINE HER DOING THAT...

KYAAA♥

BUT...I GUESS...

I WOULDN'T COMPLAIN, BUT...

I'D PROBABLY GET REALLY LONELY...

I KNOW, RIGHT?!

THAT'S IT!

THAT'S WHAT I'M TALKING ABOUT!

WHAT *ARE* YOU TALKING ABOUT?

AHAHA!

Trouble Brewing

HIS AURA IS COMPLETELY DIFFERENT.

GOD, HE'S GOTTEN CUTER...

SPARKLE

SPARKLE

O-M-G! HE LOOKS SO GOOD TODAY!

H-HERE COMES MISAKI-SENPAI!

ALL RIGHT, LET'S GO!

WE NEED HIM TO NOTICE US...

LET'S TALK TO HIM.

BA-THUMP

BA-THUMP

BA-THUMP

BA-THUMP

IT'S HEARTBREAKING ONLY WATCHING HIM FROM AFAR!

I can't take it!

AIZAWA-SAN!

TMP

OH!

M-M-MISAKI-SENPA--

H-HEY!

......

IT'S ABOUT CLUB TODAY...

OH, WELL...

HEY, MISAKI-SENPAI! HOW'S IT HANGING?

Rival Spotted!

IT SOUNDS LIKE THEY'RE IN A CLUB TOGETHER. *Hee hee...*

BUT...

HE'S PRETTY HOT.

WE LOOKED UP ALL OF SENPAI'S FRIENDS...

WHO'S THAT? I DON'T KNOW HIM.

WHADDYA MEAN ...?

HUH?

LOOK DOWN!

LOOK!

H-HOLD ON!

SHOVE!!

HOW DARE SHE!!

WAIT, THAT'S A GIRL?

DUN!!

DUN

HE'S WEARING A SKIRT!

WHAT A BITCH!!

BOING

AND HER TITS ARE HUGE!!

Early Trepidations

BEHIND THE GYM.

WE'VE GOTTA TALK. MEET US AFTER SCHOOL.

I'M OGAWA, SAME CLASS.

I'M MIFUNE FROM CLASS B.

HEY, YOU'RE AIZAWA-SAN FROM CLASS A, RIGHT?

NOT HERE TO MAKE FRIENDS.

KINDA FEELS LIKE YOU'RE...

......

SO ARE YOU READY FOR A **REAL** SMACK-DOWN?

WHAT?!

FLINCH

HUH?!

FLINCH

BUT I DON'T LIKE GETTING DRAGGED INTO HALF-ASSED FIGHTS.

I DON'T KNOW WHAT YOUR PROBLEM IS...

SHE'S TERRI-FYING!!

YEAH...

WHAT'S WITH THIS GIRL...?!

TREMBLE

B-BRING IT ON...

TREMBLE

HEY.

I ASKED YOU IF YOU'RE READY.

TREMBLE

TREMBLE

TREMBLE

Deep Trouble

LET'S ASK THE KARATE CLUB GIRLS IN OUR CLASS ABOUT HER.

I BET IT'S ALL AN ACT.

Ha ha

C-CALM DOWN...

Grab

SHE'S TOUGH AND IN THE KARATE CLUB!

SHE'S BAD NEWS...

AI...

TWITCH

A-AIZAWA-SAN?!

I KNOW HER...

AIZAWA-SAN?

THAT STRONG?

IS SHE...

SHOCK

SHE'S SHAKIN' LIKE A LEAF...

YOU FOUGHT HER THAT ONE TIME.

There, there.

OH, RIGHT.

SHE'S TERRIFYING...

TREMBLE

TREMBLE

SHE'S WORSE THAN SHE LOOKS!!

IT'S NOT FOR SHOW AT ALL!!

TREMBLE

HAVE EVER BEATEN HER, EITHER.

AND N-NONE OF THE BOYS...

SHE'S IN THE MEN'S CLUB NOW.

SUPER STRONG.

TREMBLE

TREMBLE

TREMBLE

Danger! Danger! Danger!

She might be strong but that doesn't mean you're going to get punched, all right?!

We can't do something lame like that now!

SOB!

I don't want to get hit!

We should apologize!!

Clench

SOB!

I WAS SHAKING SO BAD, SHE KEPT APOLOGIZING TO ME AFTER THE MATCH...

YEAH...

I GUESS SHE'S JUST NORMAL?

WELL...

MEAN OR NICE?!

WHAT'S HER PERSONALITY LIKE?

YOU'RE GOING TO FIGHT HER?!

NO, NO! OF C-COURSE NOT...

Y-YOU DIDN'T...

WHAT ?!

SOOOO... IF SOMEONE KINDA ACCIDENTALLY PICKED A FIGHT WITH HER...WOULD SHE PUNCH THEM?

WE'VE GOTTA APOLOGIZE!!

I'M... GOING TO DIE...

Wobble

DIE ...?

PROBABLY DIE.

I-IF I GOT IN A REAL FIGHT WITH HER... I'D...

IT'D BE BAD... I HEARD SHE'S ALWAYS FIGHTING THE BOYS IN HER CLASS...

Wobble

TREMBLE

TREMBLE

Minor Concussions at Most

I DIDN'T DO ANY- THING! AND WHAT DO YOU MEAN, "THIS TIME"?

WHAT DID YOU DO THIS TIME?

SO THESE TWO CHICKS WANT TO FIGHT ME...

What a drag...

SIGH...

"TUSSLE," YOU SAID.

HOLD IT RIGHT THERE.

I GUESS I'M A GIRL TOO, SO IT'S FINE, BUT...

THINKING ABOUT IT, THIS IS MY FIRST TUSSLE WITH GIRLS.

ARE YOU SERIOUSLY PLANNING TO PUNCH TWO GIRLS?

HUH?

I MEAN WE'RE GONNA FIGHT.

WHAT DO YOU MEAN BY TUSSLE?

THAT'S NOT THE ISSUE HERE.

I'LL GO EASY ON 'EM!

I'M NO SADIST.

Ha ha ha!

No Law Against Misuzu's Approach

I MEAN, THEY SHOULD FOLD AFTER ONE PUNCH EACH--

YOU DON'T GET IT.

CLENCH

I WASN'T PLANNING ON BEING THEIR FRIEND ONCE THEY PICKED A FIGHT!

WELL, DUH.

HIGH SCHOOL GIRLS DON'T MAKE FRIENDS WITH THEIR FISTS.

SET-TLE DOWN.

WELL, YES, BUT...

BUT I'M **CRAP** AT THAT!

THEY WANT TO FIGHT YOU WITH WORDS.

THEY'RE PROB-ABLY ALREADY SCARED!

NO EXCUSES!

B-BUT...

IF YOU WANT TO FIGHT THEM, YOU NEED TO DO IT ON THEIR TERMS.

Got it?

YOU CAN'T JUST PUNCH THEM.

YOU'RE MORE TERRIFY-ING THAN I AM...

I WILL MAKE SURE THEIR HIGH SCHOOL LIFE IS HELL.

BUT IF THEY DO SAY ANYTHING REALLY MEAN TO YOU, TELL ME.

Gwo Gwo Gwo Gwo Gwo...

Choose Your Words Carefully...

So That's What This is About

WHAT? W-WELL...

SHAKE

SHAKE

WHAT'S THAT GOT TO DO WITH ME?

HAVE THIS GUY WE LIKE...

Y-YOU SEE... WE...

TWITCH!!

WE LIKE MISAKI-SENPAI!

SO *THAT'S* WHAT THIS IS ABOUT.

HUH?

I GET IT.

AND...

Shff.

WE SAW YOU WITH HIM... YOU TWO WERE LAUGH-ING AND CHAT-TING...

WHY DOES SHE LOOK SO HAPPY?!

WHAT?! WHAT'S GOING ON?!

YOU SHOULDA TOLD ME SOONER!

Jeez!

SO YOU WANT TO GET CLOSER TO SENPAI AND CAME TO ME FOR LOVE ADVICE?!

All right!

Dear Tomo-chan...

THAT'S NOT IT AT ALL!

IT'S NOT THAT!

N-NO!

BEING ASKED FOR THAT... IT'S, LIKE, THE GIRLIEST THING EVER!

Heh heh heh...

I CAN'T BELIEVE SOMEBODY'S ASKING ME FOR LOVE ADVICE!

I GET IT! REALLY!

KYA!

EEK...

DON'T BE SHY!

THEN WE SHOULD TOTALLY BE FRIENDS!

SPARKLE

SPARKLE

YOU WANT SENPAI TO NOTICE YOU, RIGHT?

SHE LOOKS RELIABLE, AT LEAST.

I GUESS...

HOW'S SHE... SO STRONG...?

Y-YEAH...

I CAN BACK YOU UP.

BA-THUMP

BA-THUMP

BA-THUMP

BA-THUMP

Tomo-chan's Old Nickname

WELL, THEY WERE SO EMBARRASSED THEY RAN AWAY RIGHT AFTER.

WEREN'T THEY JUST SCARED?

IS THAT REALLY WHAT HAPPENED?

I NEVER THOUGHT IT WOULD BE LOVE ADVICE!

Nya ha ha!

I WAS SO SURE WE WERE GONNA HAVE A BRAWL!

HM...

I WONDER.

GLANCE

AND FROM FOLKS I DON'T EVEN KNOW? I MUST BE SUPER GIRLY!

Nya Ha ha ha!

HA! THIS MEANS THERE'S NO MISTAKING I'M A GIRL NOW! ♪

HUH?

NO, I DON'T.

DO YOU KNOW WHAT PEOPLE CALLED YOU BEHIND YOUR BACK IN JUNIOR HIGH?

STARE....

HEY, TOMO.

I'VE NEVER KILLED ANYONE!

WHAT?

THE AIR-HEADED LADY KILLER.

That's the Face of a Woman

A Violent Embrace

DEFI-NITELY!

SO AIZAWA-SAN LIKES THAT GUY.

SHE'S KINDA IMMATURE.

TOO FUNNY!

SHE WENT BRIGHT RED JUST WHEN HE PUT HIS ARM AROUND HER!

Pkk!

Pkk!

WHATCHA TALKIN' 'BOUT?

GLOMP

HEY, GUYS!

?!

?!

OH, MY BAD...

HUH?

YOU SCARED US!

Eek!

Eek!

D-DON'T JUMP US LIKE THAT!

How is it?

We let our hair down...

On the Bus Home

Hand of Darkness

WHY AM I THE ONE BLUSHING LIKE A SELF-CONSCIOUS IDIOT?

DAMN! JUN LOOKS SO CALM.

?

HUH...?

CREEP

I JUST WANT HIM TO TREAT ME LIKE A GIRL...

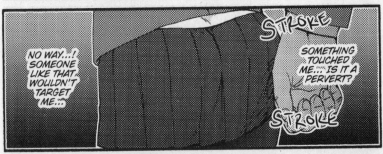

NO WAY...! SOMEONE LIKE THAT WOULDN'T TARGET ME...

STROKE

SOMETHING TOUCHED ME... IS IT A PERVERT?

STROKE

HE'S GROPING ME?!

GROPE

The Unnoticed Demon

I'M GONNA PUNCH HIS LIGHTS OUT!!

WAIT...

TCH ....!

GRIT

CREEP CREEP

DAMN IT... SO THIS GUY'S FINE WITH ANY OLD HIGH SCHOOL GIRL?!

I-IT'S NOTHING!

RE-ALLY?

Aha ha!

HUH?! OH, NO...

WHAT'S UP? YOU LOOK PISSED.

HEY, TOMO...

HM?

WHY. DON'T. I WANT JUN TO KNOW...?

AHA HA HA...

WHAT THE...? WHY?

What (Not) to Say Next

THAT'S A LITTLE MUCH.

LOCK HIM UP FOR LIFE.

Aw...

JUN TOOK CARE OF EVERYTHING, FROM REPORTING IT TO HANDING HIM OVER.

WHAT DO I DO? I CAN'T LOOK HIM IN THE FACE.

AND YOU SHOULD...

WE SHOULD GO TO THE POLICE LATER. It'll be a pain, but still...

THIS IS THE FIRST TIME HE'S TREATED ME LIKE A GIRL.

WH-WHAT?!

I WAS JUST SAYING...

FLINCH

HUH?!

YOU LISTENING?

HEY!

BWA-HUH?

MAYBE YOU SHOULD STOP WEARING SKIRTS?

Skirting the Issue

The Important Part

SO, I RAN INTO A MOLESTER YESTERDAY... LISTEN TO THIS, MISUZU.

AND THAT IDIOT JUN...

WHAT DID YOU JUST SAY?

HUH?

THAT JUN...

I DON'T CARE ABOUT HIM!

S-SNAP

WHAT'S THIS ABOUT A MOLESTER? DID HE TOUCH YOU? ARE YOU OKAY?

Y-YEAH.

HE GROPED MY BUTT A LITTLE...

DID YOU TURN HIM OVER TO THE POLICE? HE DIDN'T GET AWAY, DID HE?

J-JUN DID ALL THAT.

OKAY.

HUH? MISU-ZU?

Jeez...!

Phew...!

WELL...

≶FLINCH

ERR...

WHAT ABOUT JUN?

SO?

I WAS SO FRICKIN' PISSED I PUNCHED HIM!

HEH. NICE.

SO *THAT'S* WHY YOU'RE UPSET.

THAT MORON JUN TOLD ME NOT TO WEAR SKIRTS ANYMORE!

RE-ALLY?!

DO YOU THINK HE ACTUALLY THINKS OF ME LIKE THAT?

HUH?!

BA-THUMP

BUT HE MAY HAVE SAID THAT TO PROTECT YOU FROM BEING GROPED AGAIN.

・・・・・・・

・・・・・・・

CAN'T YOU AT LEAST SAY "MAYBE"?!

WHAT?!

I'M SORRY... I DON'T KNOW WHAT I WAS THINKING.

HUH?

WHAT ABOUT IT?

YOUR SKIRT...

I WAS WONDERING THIS BEFORE, BUT...

BUT IT'S OKAY TO WEAR IT THIS SHORT IN HIGH SCHOOL. I couldn't in junior high.

OHH...

IT'S SURPRISINGLY SHORT.

WHY...?

WHY DO YOU WEAR IT SO SHORT?

YOU DON'T SEEM LIKE THE TYPE OF PERSON WHO LIKES TO SHOW OFF THEIR LEGS.

YOU REALLY AREN'T SUITED TO SKIRTS.

WHY ELSE?

IT MAKES IT EASIER TO MOVE.

Tomo-chan's Ethics

DON'T BE LEWD!

HUH ?!

NO WAY !!

EITHER WAY, WHY DON'T YOU TRY *NOT* WEARING YOUR SHORTS TODAY?

I'M NOT BEING LEWD.

SHOVE

IF YOUR SKIRT GETS LIFTED UP, EVERYONE CAN SEE EVERYTHING!

IS NORMAL.

NO WAY!

TOMO-CHAN, WEARING A SKIRT WITH JUST UNDERWEAR...

THAT'S WHAT WORRIES YOU?

BUT I'M ONLY WEARING UNDERWEAR TODAY.

I SOMETIMES WEAR BLACK OR NAVY-BLUE SHORTS.

DON'T GIVE ME THAT LOOK.

UGH...

Step

OHH. SO YOU'RE INTO BEING WATCHED ...?

Convincing Her Took Forever

He Started Walking Funny

Different from What I Imagined

I ENDED UP DOING WHAT MISUZU SAID.

It's breezy...

I'M SURE JUNICHIRO WILL SEE YOU DIFFERENTLY!

ANYWAY, TRY GOING WITHOUT THEM, JUST ONCE.

......

MY BAD! SORRY!

HEY, JUN... ABOUT PUNCHING YOU SO HARD YESTERDAY...

BUT JUN'S ACTING DIFFERENT.

WHP

HEY!

I DON'T KNOW IF IT'S BECAUSE I'M NOT WEARING SHORTS...

HE'S ACTING REALLY WEIRD!!

JUN?!

JUMP

GO

ACK!

NG

ACTUALLY...

The Bodyguard

Up!

Down

First Win?

I'M SORRY ABOUT YESTERDAY.

HUH?

YOU'VE BEEN KINDA WEIRD TODAY.

YOU OKAY?

Hey...

IT DOESN'T MATTER THAT YOU'RE MY BEST FRIEND, I HAD NO RIGHT TO TELL YOU WHAT YOU WEAR.

I WAS WAY OUTTA LINE.

WHAT?

IT WAS MY OWN...

IS-SUES...

I SHOULDN'T HAVE ACTED IN A WAY THAT EMBARRASSED YOU MORE.

EVEN LISTEN-ING TO ME?

ARE YOU...

Wow!

I'VE NEVER SEEN JUN MAKE THAT FACE BEFORE!

Inexplicable

Time to Reset

SHE'S REALLY LONELY.

SHUT UP.

LOOKS LIKE YOU DIDN'T SPEAK TO TOMO AT ALL THIS MORNING.

YOU HAVING TROUBLE *RESETTING* THIS TIME?

IT'S NOT LIKE YOU TO AVOID HER FOR HALF A DAY.

LEAN...

FLICK

JUST TRY--

Back to Normal, Right?

PHEW... ......

AAH...

LET'S GRAB LUNCH!

WHOA! JUN!

SQUEEZE

MORNIN', TOMO~!

IT'LL BE FUN TO WATCH!

I WONDER HOW LONG THEY CAN KEEP UP THIS CHARADE.

AWW! MEANIE!

DON'T JUMP ME LIKE THAT!

OMAKE

Color Commentary

FLINCH

ASH GRAY...

I BELIEVE YESTERDAY WAS...

......

SKIES ALL DAY.

......

WELL...

I SUPPOSE IT WAS MORE A LIGHT GRAY.

GET LOST.

HEY.

FIFTY SHADES OF GRAY?

OR MAYBE SILVER GRAY? SMOKEY GRAY?

TOMO-CHAN
IS A GIRL!

School Idol

BOUNCE BOUNCE

WANT ME TO CARRY IT?

YOUR BAG LOOKS HEAVY.

YOU'RE AS CUTE AS EVER!

MORNING, CAROL-CHAN!

LA DI DA!♪

OKAY.

MORN-ING!

CHATTER CHATTER

SHE'S ALWAYS GOT A CROWD OF GUYS AROUND HER.

It's impressive!

AND HERE SHE COMES. CAROL OLSTON.

WHO KNOWS?

THEN THAT WOULD MAKE HER THE GIRLIEST?

SO, IF SHE'S THE MOST POPULAR WITH THE GUYS...

Right?

MAYBE START BY PUTTING DOWN THE DUMB-BELL.

WELL...

CLENCH

WHAT DO I HAVE TO DO TO BE LIKE THAT?

MUST BE NICE.

CLENCH

A Girl Junichiro Complimented

THAT'S CALLED "ADMIRING."

I JUST THOUGHT IT'D BE NICE TO BE LIKE HER.

IT'S NOT LIKE THAT...

STILL, IT'S NOT OFTEN YOU ADMIRE OTHER GIRLS.

CLAP

THAT CAN'T BE RIGHT. TELL ME THE WHOLE STORY.

JUN-ICHIRO COMPLI-MENTED HER?

SHE'S THE ONLY GIRL JUN'S EVER COMPLI-MENTED.

FINE, I AM KINDA JEALOUS.

IT'S LIKE A WALKING MANNE-QUIN!

La la la! ♪

HUH?

HEY, LOOK AT THAT, TOMO!

REALLY A COMPLI-MENT?

WAS THAT...

THAT'S WHAT HE SAID.

Dammit, Jun...

It's About Character

Suddenly Carol

COTTON CANDY

La La La

COULD I UNDERSTAND IF I MADE FRIENDS WITH THAT COTTON-CANDY GIRL?

Hmm...

WHAT DID SHE MEAN, IT'S BETTER TO BE DEFENSE-LESS?

I don't get women...

OH, MISAKI-SENPAI...

YOU LOOK SO SERIOUS! WHAT'S UP?

HI AIZAWA-SAN!

Fluffy

?

ABOUT...?

I WAS JUST THINK-ING...

COTTON CANDY?!

COTTON CANDY?

Jolt

COT--!!

COTTON CANDY!!!

Culture Shock

FIANCÉE?!

I'M HIS FIANCÉE!

SHE'S A DISTANT RELATIVE OF MINE. WE'RE CHILDHOOD FRIENDS.

OH, YOU MEAN CAROL?

WHAT'S SHE DOING HERE ...?

YOU TWO ARE GONNA TO GET MARRIED WHEN YOU GROW UP?!

MAYBE...

WELL, IF MY FAMILY HAD THEIR WAY...

S-SERIOUSLY?!

THREE TIMES NOW.

WE'VE ALREADY GOTTEN MARRIED.

WHOA, AIZAWA-SAN! THOSE WERE JUST MAKE-BELIEVE WEDDINGS WE DID BACK WHEN WE WERE KIDS...

IS THAT HOW IT'S DONE IN ENGLAND?!

THREE TIMES... YOU CAN DO THAT?!

Off the Radar

If She's a Girl...

Every Now and Then

HEY, STUPID HEAD!

CLOP

CLOP

BEATS ME...

WHAT'S THAT ABOUT?

THAT'S THE THIRD TIME TODAY.

She Can't Help It

SO THAT'S THEIR RELATIONSHIP.

I SEE.

SEEMS SHE'S MISAKI-SENPAI'S CHILDHOOD FRIEND AND FIANCÉE.

Not wife yet, though.

TODAY WAS THE FIRST TIME I EVER SPOKE TO HER.

YEAH, HE WAS.

HUH?

WAS SENPAI THERE WHEN YOU TALKED TO HER?

NO CLUE.

NOPE.

AND YOU DON'T KNOW WHY SHE STARTED CALLING YOU STUPID FROM THAT?

OH MY GOD, NOT YOU TOO!!!

STUPID HEAD.

Gundou Misuzu's Strategy

YOU'RE RIGHT.

I'M NO GOOD AT DEALING WITH GIRLS...

SO SHE'S GOT A PROBLEM WITH ME. WHAT SHOULD I DO?

BUT, TOMO'S NOT. GOING TO UNDERSTAND ANY OF THEM...

IF SHE'S MISAKI'S FIANCÉE, THERE ARE A FEW WAYS TO HANDLE THIS.

I WONDER IF THEY'VE HEARD...

OH!

DO THEY KNOW ABOUT HIS FIANCÉE?

BY THE WAY, YOU KNOW TWO FANS OF MISAKI-SENPAI.

YOU'RE RIGHT...

YEAH...

OF COURSE.

THEY'LL FIND OUT EVENTUALLY...

IT MIGHT BE HARD ON THEM...BUT YOU SHOULD LET THEM KNOW.

Bearing the Bad News

WH-WHAT DO YOU WANT?!

JOLT

AIZAWA TOMO!!!

JOLT

WAH!

HEY, GUYS. YOU GOT A SEC?

OH... WELL...

WHO?!

KYAA

WE'VE NEVER HEARD THAT!!

GWAH!

MISAKI-SENPAI HAS A FIAN-CÉE?!

HUH?!

YOU KNOW HER?

SOME CHICK NAMED **CAROL**. SHE'S IN MY CLASS.

YEAH, I CAN SEE THAT...

SHE'S THE WORST.

GLOOM

OHHHH... HER...

Total Defeat

WHY AM I HERE?

SO LISTEN UP!

WE'VE GOT SOMETHING TO SAY TO YOU.

WHAT DID YOU WANT TO TALK ABOUT?

READ THE ROOM!!

THAT'S NOT IT AT ALL!!!

WHY WOULD WE WANT THAT?!

YOU WANT TO BE MY FRIEND?

......

WE WEREN'T ASKING—

G-G-G?! SERI-OUSLY?!

G?!

BIG-BOOBED? MY BOOBS ARE G-CUP.

Argh!

LISTEN UP, YOU BIG-BOOBED BIMBO!

DON'T INTRO-DUCE YOUR-SELF!!

MY NAME IS CAROL.

Nice to meet you!

Arrgh!

YOU TRIED YOUR BEST...

SHE'S... I CAN'T EVEN...

I CAN'T TALK TO HER.

LET'S BE FRIENDS!

Ten Minutes Later...

PAT

SOB!

SOB!

Kneeling Makes Me Look Humble, Right?

YOU'RE TOMO-CHAN'S FRIEND, AREN'T YOU, MISUZU-CHAN?

MISUZU-CHAAN~!

ALWAYS HAVE BEEN.

THAT'S RIGHT.

YEAH.

BUT FIRST...

OKAY.

I WANT TO TALK TO YOU ABOUT SOME-THING.

OKAY~!

GET OFF MY DESK.

Everyone Has Their Price

STUBBORN, AREN'T YOU?

SO, CAN WE TALK NOW?

OKAY, COOL!

I NEED YOU TO UNDERSTAND SOMETHING: I DON'T LIKE PEOPLE LIKE YOU.

YOU THINK OF TOMO AS A RIVAL, RIGHT?

I'M NOT SURPRISED.

I WANT TO ASK ABOUT TOMO-CHAN.

IF YOU WANT TO KNOW HER WEAKNESS, GO ASK SOMEONE ELSE.

BUT FRIENDS DON'T SELL OUT FRIENDS.

FRIENDSHIP IS OVERRATED.

. . . . . .

EVEN IF I GAVE YOU CAKE?

Double chocolate?

Where Does She Fit In?

COULD AT LEAST *TRY* TO BE SUBTLE.

YOU...

HOW CAN I CRUSH TOMO-CHAN?

S000...

NOW THEN.... HOW CAN I USE HER...?

THERE'S SOMEONE WHO KNOWS HER EVEN BETTER THAN ME.

ACTU-ALLY...

GO ASK A BOY NAMED KUBOTA JUN-ICHIRO.

That's What You Want?

WHAT'S SHE UP TO...?

IT WAS GUNDOU, WASN'T IT?

AND SOMEONE TOLD ME I SHOULD TALK TO YOU ABOUT IT.

I WANT TO BEAT SOMEONE...

I DIDN'T THINK ANY GIRL BESIDES TOMO WOULD SAY SHE WANTS TO BEAT SOMEONE.

I DON'T CARE IF SHE CAME BECAUSE GUNDOU SUGGESTED IT, BUT...

I NEEDED TO KILL TIME WHILE MY FRIEND FINISHES HER CLUB ANYWAYS.

I SEE. ALL RIGHT THEN.

I WANT YOU TO TEACH ME!

TRAIN?

I'LL TRAIN YOU AFTER SCHOOL.

IF YOU'RE ALL RIGHT WITH IT...

Both Animals Are Babies

I MEANT MY **HAND,** BUT YEAH.

LIKE THIS?

PLAP

I WANT YOU TO HIT ME AS HARD AS YOU CAN.

MEW!

LIKE A KITTEN?!

WEAKER THAN A KITTEN.

STILL, YOU'RE AMAZINGLY FEEBLE...

IF WE HAD A **MONTH,** THEN MAYBE...

WELL...

YOU'VE GOT SPUNK, BUT...

CAN YOU MAKE ME STRONGER?

RARR!!

IS THAT STRONG?

YOU'D BE AS STRONG AS A BABY BEAR.

Afterschool Shock

LET'S GO, BLONDIE.

HEY.

I'M CAROL~!

CLOP CLOP

I'M NOT BLONDIE!

JUST HURRY UP.

OKAY~!

WELL, *THAT* HAP-PENED.

Paranoia Creeps In

SHAKE SHAKE

DUNNO. Calm down.

WHY ARE JUN AND THAT GIRL...?!

DID YOU SEE THAT?! WHAT THE HELL?!

I'VE NEVER SEEN JUNICHIRO TALK TO ANY GIRL BUT YOU LIKE THAT...

HOW-EVER...

SOME-THING MUST'VE HAP-PENED.

ACK ...!!!

DU DU DUUN

MAYBE THE TWO OF THEM ARE...

YOU'RE NOT USED TO THIS KIND OF DREAD.

THAT'S IT, TOMO...

NO... BUT... WHAT IF...

PLIP

PLIP

NO... IT CAN'T BE. SHE HAS A FIANCE.

Her Power Level

She Can't Go Easy on Them

Getting to the Starting Line

ALL RIGHT, LET'S START BY JOGGING TO THE SCHOOL GATE.

YUP~!

GOOD, YOU GOT CHANGED.

THE CLUBS ARE USING THE FIELD AND GYM.

THD

THD

CLOP

CLOP

WE'RE GOING OUTSIDE THE SCHOOL?

Wait~!

NOW, LET'S RUN TWICE AROUND THE SCHOOL GROUNDS...

GOOD WARM-UP.

ALL RIGHT.

YOU'RE KIDDING, RIGHT?

WHEW~!

I'M ALL TUCKERED OUT!

WHAT'S WRONG?

Awe-Inspiring Weakness

Beats me...

What're they doing?

OKAY~!

NEXT IS MUSCLE TRAINING. WE'LL HAVE TO USE THE CORNER OF THE GYM FOR THIS.

I CAN'T.

Silence~...

ONE...

FIRST THE ABS.

NO GOOD.

Silence~...

ONE...

THEN PUSH-UPS.

THE BOARD GAME?

I'M GREAT AT OTHELLO!

WHAT CAN YOU DO?

Stretching out of Trouble

I DON'T GET WHAT YOU'RE SAYING, BUT GO AHEAD.

ALL RIGHT.

I LOVE BUNNIES!

I CAN JUMP ROPE!

SO SLOW...

HUP!

BOUNCE

BOUNCE

HUP!

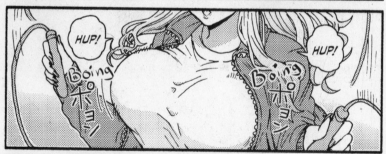

HUP!

HUP!

NECK EXERCISES.

WHY ARE YOU LOOKING UP?

OH?

At Least Stop the Jiggling

WE DID LIKE ONE-FIFTH OF THE EXERCISES I'D PLANNED.

FINALLY! I THOUGHT I WAS GONNA DIE.

Whew!

WE DON'T HAVE MUCH TIME, SO LET'S STOP THE MUSCLE TRAINING.

DON'T SAY THAT WORD.

MY BREASTS?

DO SOMETHING ABOUT THOSE...

ALSO, YOU SHOULD...

WHY?

I'M GETTING DISTRACTED.

WHY ARE YOU LOOKING OVER THERE?

DON'T THEY GET IN THE WAY?

YOU'RE FUNNY!

Also, no way.

YOU NEED TO FLATTEN THOSE.

ANYWAY, IF YOU WANT TO WIN...

She Got Here in a Hurry

I JUST FINISHED CLUB, LET'S GO HOME...

Ran all over school.

SO THIS IS WHERE YOU WERE...

H-HEY, JUN!

HAAH! HAAH!

YEAH.

WHEN YOUR OPPONENT DOES THIS...

GOT IT?

TWITCH

ACK...

AGH!

IT REALLY WAS TOMO...

Strong like a gorilla?

THAT'S HER!

OH! Found you!

SHAKE

WH-WHAT...

SHAKE

DUNNO.

WHAT IS SHE MAD ABOUT?

GRRRAH!!

WHAT ARE YOU TWO DOING?!!

Huh?

…… | I'M NOT MAD! I'M JUST ASKING! | WHY'RE YOU MAD…? | H-HEY. | TWITCH TWITCH | I ASKED YOU A QUESTION!

OH, I SEE!

Nice play, Mishuzu-chan~

IF YOU'RE NOT A COMPLETE IDIOT, THAT IS.

YOU'LL UNDER-STAND IF YOU KEEP HANGING AROUND THAT BOY.

HUH?

ERR…

PATT PATT

I'M GOING TO STOP BEING YOUR RIVAL!

TOMO-CHAN! TOMO-CHAN!

BYEEE!

CLOP CLOP

I QUIT TRAIN-ING, TOO~!

Moving Evaluation

I CAME ALONG BECAUSE YOU PROMISED ME CAKE, BUT...

LOOK...

EX-CUSE ME?

YOU GOT ME, MISUZU-CHAN~!

So mean~!

SИООTH

HUH?

I DON'T KNOW.

YOU CALLED FOR IT.

WHY THE FLASHY LIMO?

· · · · · ·

I DON'T KNOW HIS NAME.

HIM?

YOU CALLED HIM.

HE DOESN'T SEEM LIKE YOUR FATHER.

AND WHO'S THE GUY IN THE BLACK SUIT?

MOST PEOPLE DON'T.

DON'T YOU HAVE ANY, MISUZU-CHAN?

I DON'T REMEM-BER THEIR NAMES. THERE ARE SO MANY MEN IN SUITS AT HOME.

Surprising Knowledge

Friend Bequest

TOMO-CHAN?

I'M SURE SHE'LL ACCEPT.

DING-A-LING

YOU SHOULD ASK TOMO TO BE YOUR FRIEND.

I DID A LOT OF REALLY MEAN THINGS TO TOMO-CHAN.

BUT...

I SEE.

I'LL LEND HER TO YOU, BUT ONLY FOR A BIT.

SHE MIGHT HELP MOTIVATE TOMO, TOO.

SHE EVEN CALLS SOME-ONE LIKE ME HER FRIEND.

SHE'S ONE OF THE KINDEST PEOPLE YOU'LL EVER MEET.

LOOK, DON'T WORRY ABOUT THAT.

YOU'RE ONE TO TALK.

THAT'S AMAZING SINCE YOU'RE REALLY MEAN, MISUZU-CHAN.

WOW~!

It's Hard to Say

YOU! WHAT NOW?

HUH?

Fluffy

HEY, HEY, TOMO-CHAN!

Let's be friends!

Let's be fwends...

WELL...

ACK!!

FLINCH

A LITTLE HARD TO SAY...

ERM... THIS IS...

WHAT COULD BE SO BAD THAT EVEN SHE'D HESITATE?!

SHE'S USUALLY SO BLUNT AND MEAN!

BA-THUMP

BA-THUMP

Friendship's Charms

GOOD FOR YOU.

YEAH!

TOMO-CHAN REALLY IS MY FRIEND NOW!

It worked!

MISUZU-CHAN~!

RE-ALLY?!

I SUPPOSE.

WILL *YOU* BE MY FRIEND TOO, MISUZU-CHAN?

IT'S GOOD TO HAVE RICH FRIENDS.

BUT ONLY BE-CAUSE...

SMIRK

SMILE

IT'S TRUE! I'M TOTALLY LOADED!

WHOO-HOO! YAY!

Jun-kun Options

Un-Bear-Able So Far

Didn't Think I'd Hear That Name Here

......

WE LUCKED OUT.

Jackpot!

I KNOW!

THERE ARE SOME GOOD ONES....

THE FIRST-YEARS?

WHAT DO YOU THINK OF THE FIRST-YEAR GIRLS?

BOR-ING.

SERI-OUS-LY?!

MY JAW DROPPED SOON AS I SAW HER AT THE ENTRANCE CEREMONY.

YEAH, SHE'S GORGEOUS.

She's like a doll.

CAROL IS SUCH A HOTTIE!

I WONDER WHAT TOMO'S UP TO.

Music class, I think?

IDIOT! THAT'S WHAT'S GREAT ABOUT HER!

You don't get it!

SHE'S CUTE BUT...SHE IGNORED ME COMPLETELY WHEN I TRIED TO TALK TO HER.

She's kinda scary.

OH MAN! MISUZU-CHAN IS FRICKIN' ADORABLE!

WHAT ABOUT GUNDOU-SAN, EH?

HUH ?!

I KNOW! SHE REALLY ROCKS THE SEXY TOMBOY LOOK.

AIZAWA-SAN'S HOT! WHAT A GREAT BODY.

THEN THERE'S AIZAWA-SAN!

130

You Said He Was Cool

131

I Didn't Think I'd Hear That Name Either

OUR OPTIONS SUCK THIS YEAR!

YEAH.

THEY'RE NOTHING SPECIAL.

THE FIRST-YEARS?

WHAT DO YOU THINK OF THE FIRST-YEAR BOYS?

· · · · · · · ·

I WONDER WHAT JUN'S UP TO...

I think he's in gym.

BOR-ING...

REAL-LY?!

ISN'T HE, LIKE, ONE-QUARTER BRITISH?

His eyes are blue.

HE IS! ♡ HIS FACE LOOKS LIKE ANGELS CARVED IT, AND I HEARD HE'S SUPER KIND.

BUT MIZUKI-SENPAI IS **AMAZING**, RIGHT? ♡

?!

I HEARD HE HAS QUITE THE BODY.

The boys were being loud about it.

OH YEAH! HE'S KINDA SCARY BUT ALSO COOL AND HAND-SOME.

IF I HAD TO PICK A FIRST-YEAR...I GUESS KUBOTA-KUN?

SLUMP

Shh! Keep it down! She's right there!

She'll hear you!

YEAH! TOO BAD SHE'S A GIRL!

A shame!

THEN THERE'S **AIZAWA-SAN!** ♡

It's Creepy

APPAR-ENTLY.

People suck.

JUN IS REALLY POPULAR WITH GIRLS.

LISTEN TO THIS, MISUZU.

DON'T YOU LIKE HIM?

I DON'T GET IT.

BUT... IT'S JUN.

REAL-LY?!

I GUESS IT MAKES HIM LOOK COOL AND STOIC.

HE MOSTLY WEARS A SOUR EXPRESSION WITH ANYONE THAT'S NOT YOU.

Ugly!

BUT IT'S CREEPY HEARING OTHER GIRLS CALL HIM COOL AND HAND-SOME AND STUFF.

ERM... WELL, I GUESS...

YOU NEED TO TELL HIM TO KNOCK THAT OFF.

Stop it!

MWA HA HA!!

IS COOL... AND HAND-SOME?

TICKLE

TICKLE

THAT CHILDISH BRAT WHO LIKES TO TICKLE ME AND KNOCK OUT MY KNEES...

133

Comfort Zone

WHY DO YOU LIKE HIM?

NOT THAT I'M GOING TO **ENJOY** THE ANSWER, BUT...

WH-WHY...?

THAT'S USUALLY A DEAL-BREAKER.

IGNORING THE FACT THAT HE TREATS ME LIKE A DUDE...

Ha ha...

I GET THAT YOU HATE HIM BUT HE'S ACTUALLY A REALLY NICE GUY, YOU KNOW?

UGH...

I DON'T REALLY HAVE A REASON...

HOW DO I PUT IT...?

THERE ARE A LOT OF GOOD THINGS TOO...

SURE, A LOT ABOUT HIM PISSES ME OFF, BUT...

BLUSH...

YOU ARE COMPATIBLE LIKE THAT.

THAT'S TRUE.

I FEEL COMFORTABLE PUNCHING.

AND... HE'S THE ONLY GUY...

CLENCH

I Do Bench Presses, But Still...

RE-ALLY?

SUPER GIRLY AND REALLY CUTE!

WELL, THOSE TWO ARE...

IT SEEMS BLONDIE AND GUNDOU ARE REALLY POPULAR WITH THE GUYS.

I don't get why...

JUMP

WH-WHAT DID THEY SAY?!

HUH?!

ME?!

ACTUALLY, YOUR NAME CAME UP, TOO.

HEH HEH HEH HEH...

• • • • • •

THEY SAID...

?!

MY PECS?!

Weird!!

YOU HAVE GREAT PECS.

News Flash

DON'T TELL ME YOU LIKE MISUZU?!

HELL NO.

WHA ...?!

I CAN'T REALLY JUDGE PEOPLE FOR PRE- FERRING GUNDOU...

OH...

WE DID DATE BRIEFLY.

BUT BACK IN JUNIOR HIGH...

WHO- OPS!

WHAT?

....

BONUS CONTENT

But She's in the Men's Club

WHY DID YOU JOIN THE KARATE CLUB?

HEY...

LET'S GO HOME ONCE I'M DONE WITH CLUB.

HUH?

THAT'S NOT TRUE...

WELL...

THERE'S NEVER BEEN ANYONE AS GOOD AS YOU, SO WHAT'S THE POINT?

Ha ha...

WHEN IT COMES TO BEING A WOMAN... OR JUST BEING **HUMAN.**

SMILE

I JUST CAN'T COMPETE...

I FEEL LIKE...WHEN IT COMES TO THE REALLY **IMPORTANT** THINGS...

WHAT KIND OF MONSTERS ARE IN THE GIRLS' KARATE CLUB?!

GWO GWO GWO GWO GWO

IF TOMO THINKS THAT, THEN...

My Favorite

On Second Thought

MISUZU...

TOMO...

WELL...

I SUPPOSE YOU CAN CALL ME WHATEVER YOU WANT...

RE-ALLY?

YOU CAN JUST CALL ME "CAROL" IF YOU LIKE!

WITH-OUT THE SUF-FIX?

I CAN CALL YOU THAT, RIGHT?

HEY!

MISU-ZU--

YOU'RE KINDA FLIGHTY, AREN'T YOU?

COULD YOU INCLUDE THE SUFFIX, PLEASE?

ACTU-ALLY...

Did Jun and Misuzu
really go out?!!!

Tomo and Jun finally...

have a date?!!!!

Misuzu and Carol help Tomo

coordinate her style!!

SEVEN SEAS ENTERTAINMENT PRESENTS

TOMO-CHAN IS A GIRL! Volume 1

story and art by FUMITA YANAGIDA

TRANSLATION
Jennifer O'Donnell

ADAPTATION
T Campbell

LETTERING AND RETOUCH
Carolina Hernández Mendoza

COVER DESIGN
KC Fabellon

PROOFREADER
Stephanie Cohen

EDITOR
Shannon Fay

PRODUCTION ASSISTANT
CK Russell

PRODUCTION MANAGER
Lissa Pattillo

EDITOR-IN-CHIEF
Adam Arnold

PUBLISHER
Jason DeAngelis

FOLLOW US ONLINE: www.sevenseasentertainment.com

READING DIRECTIONS

This book reads from *right to left*, Japanese style.
If this is your first time reading manga, you start
reading from the top right panel on each page and
take it from there. If you get lost, just follow the
numbered diagram here. It may seem backwards at
first, but you'll get the hang of it! Have fun!!

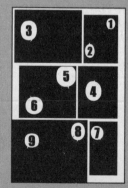